Contents

Where are the frogs and toads?

Water-holding frog

At this moment, in a desert in Australia, a frog sleeps. It is deep in a burrow under the sand. It is curled up with its eyes closed. It is waiting for the rains to fall.

Judy Allen

Frogs and
Toads

Illustrated by Steve Roberts

OXFORD
UNIVERSITY PRESS

This book belongs to

OXFORD
UNIVERSITY PRESS

Great Clarendon Street, Oxford OX2 6DP

Oxford University Press is a department of the University of Oxford.
It furthers the University's objective of excellence in research, scholarship,
and education by publishing worldwide in

Oxford New York

Athens Auckland Bangkok Bogotá Buenos Aires Calcutta
Cape Town Chennai Dar es Salaam Delhi Florence Hong Kong Istanbul
Karachi Kuala Lumpur Madrid Melbourne Mexico City Mumbai
Nairobi Paris São Paulo Singapore Taipei Tokyo Toronto Warsaw

with associated companies in Berlin Ibadan

Oxford is a registered trade mark of Oxford University Press
in the UK and in certain other countries

Hardback ISBN 0-19-910632-0
Paperback ISBN 0-19-910633-9
Pack of 6 ISBN 0-19-910757-2
Pack of 36 ISBN 0-19-910758-0

This edition is also available in Oxford Reading Tree
Branch Library Stages 8-10 Pack A

1 3 5 7 9 10 8 6 4 2

Printed and bound in Portugal by Edições ASA

Flying frog

In a jungle in Malaya, a frog flies.
It spreads out its webbed feet and
glides like a bird.
On a lake in India, a frog runs.
It runs fast on top of the water.

Midwife toad (Europe)

There are more
than 4000 kinds
of frogs and toads.

They live everywhere
in the world except the
Arctic and the Antarctic
where it is too cold.

There have been frogs
and toads on the earth
for a very long time.

Glass frog
(East Africa)

How long is a very long
time? 140 million years –
or perhaps even longer.

Frogs and toads shared the
earth with the dinosaurs.

Marsupial frog
(South America)

What are amphibians?

When the world began, the fishes and other animals lived in the oceans.

After a few million years, some animals began to climb out of the water. They learnt to breathe air. They learnt to live on land *and* in water. These animals are called amphibians.

Today, fishes live in water. So do squids and lobsters and eels and whales …

Today, animals live on land. So do birds and insects and spiders and people …

And amphibians live in water *and* on land.

frog

toad

Frogs and toads are amphibians. They can live in ponds and marshes and ditches. And they can live in gardens and fields and woods.

Frogs and toads are very
like each other. It isn't easy
to know which is which.
A good way to tell
the difference is to
look at the skin.

Most frog skins are
smooth and damp.

frog skin

Most toad skins
have bumps and
lumps, called warts.
Toad skins are not
so damp.

toad skin

Did you know...
Touching toads can make your hands
itchy and sore? **So be careful!**

Can frogs and toads sing?

Frogs and toads have ears and can hear.

Frogs and toads have voices. They can call and sing. Some croak or say, "ribbit, ribbit". Some groan or giggle, some wail or whistle.

Bullfrog

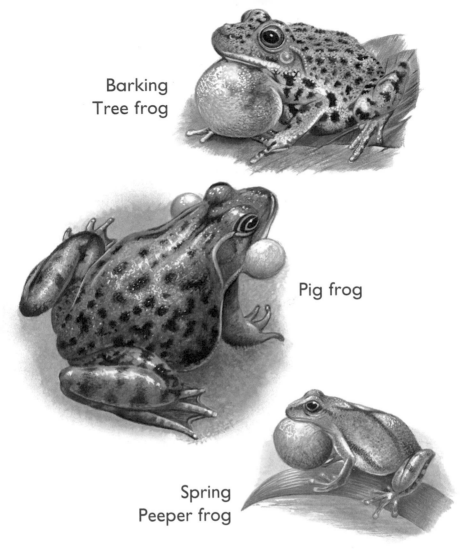

Barking
Tree frog

Pig frog

Spring
Peeper frog

Some bleat like sheep, grunt like
pigs or bark like dogs. Bullfrogs
bellow, Leopard frogs snore, and
the Spring Peeper frog sounds like
a bird singing.

Red-eyed Tree frog

Frogs and toads sing to call each other, sometimes from a long way away. So they need loud voices.

Voice sac of the Red-eyed Tree frog

A frog can puff out its throat, like a balloon. The balloon is called a voice sac. The voice sac makes the voice louder, much louder.

Some frogs sing alone.
Some frogs sing in groups.

Once, the dinosaurs heard the
frogs singing. Now, if we are lucky,
we can hear the same songs.

▶ Feet and fingers

Frogs and
toads have
strong back legs.
These help them
to swim, hop and leap.

Frogs and toads
have four fingers
and five toes.

Fingers and toes
of a frog

Some Tree frogs have
sticky pads on their toes.
This makes it easy for
them to climb.

Some frogs have webbed feet. This means they have skin between their fingers and toes.

Webbed feet help flying frogs to fly.

Webbed feet help swimming frogs to swim.

Common frog

▶ Eyes and tongues

Southern Leopard frog

Frogs and toads have large eyes.
Their eyes bulge and are on top
of their heads, so they can hide
in a pond. Only their eyes and
nose show above the water.

Frogs and toads have long tongues. Their tongues are sticky. A frog can unroll its tongue, catch a fly and flip the fly into its mouth in one second.

Frogs and toads shut their eyes when they swallow food. Their eyes sink down inside their heads and then pop out again. The large eyeballs help push down the food.

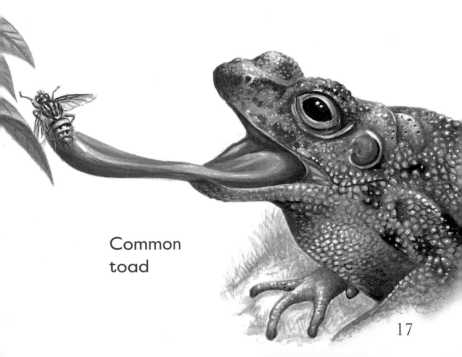

Common toad

▶ Food! Food! Food!

Frogs and toads eat insects and worms
and slugs. But big frogs and toads eat
bigger things. The African Bullfrog
eats lizards and mice. Sometimes it
will even eat a whole chicken.

African
Bullfrog

Did you know...
When a frog or a toad catches something
horrible – a spiky stag beetle or a bug
that tastes nasty – it spits it out.

▶ Eggs and tadpoles

Frogs and toads lay their eggs in water. The eggs are wrapped in jelly, to keep them warm.

Most frogs and toads lay lots of eggs.

The eggs are called spawn. Frogspawn is laid in a mass. Toadspawn is laid in strings.

Frogspawn

Toadspawn

After a while, the spawn hatches.
The young are called tadpoles.
They are tiny, no more than a
head and a tail.

Tadpoles hatching
from frogspawn

Mostly, tadpoles eat pond
slime and water plants.

They grow bigger.

They grow back legs.

Then they grow front legs.

Their tails get smaller.

▶ Danger!

The eggs and
the tadpoles are
always in danger.
They may be
eaten by fishes.
Or newts. Or ducks.

Tadpole
in danger

Or even other frogs. Sometimes,
tadpoles eat each other.

The young frogs and toads climb out
of the water.

Their stumpy tails will soon vanish.
They eat slugs and snails, worms and
insects. They grow until their skins
split – but it's all right, there's
a new skin underneath.

Grass snake
eating Common frog

But young frogs are still in
danger. They may be eaten
by ducks or herons. They may
be eaten by hedgehogs, foxes,
or snakes.

Some are eaten by humans,
and some are run over by cars
or lawnmowers.

But most of them escape. How?

They may leap out
of danger.

A Bullfrog can
leap more than
a metre.

A Common frog can
leap a long way.

They may swim out of danger.
They may hide from danger.
It's very hard to see this
Asian Leaf frog.

Asian Leaf frog

A Leopard frog
can leap nearly
two metres.

This toad has a different plan.
It puffs itself up to twice its size
in order to frighten off a snake.

Common
toad

Poison Arrow frogs

Some frogs and toads are poisonous.

The poison is on their skins.
Poisonous frogs are brightly
coloured. The bright colours
warn hungry animals to beware.

26

▶ Water matters

All frogs need water but no frogs
drink. They take in water through
their skins. All frogs need water but
they can live in very dry places.
They can even live in deserts.

The Water-holding frog of Australia
lives in the desert. It wraps itself in
slime and burrows underground. The
slime becomes firm, like packaging.
This holds water in, and keeps the
frog damp.

The Water-
holding frog
may lie like
this for two
long years.

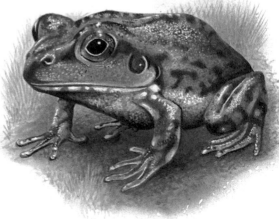

When the rainy season comes,
the frog wakes. It breaks out of
its slime-package.

The rainy season is very short, so
it must live its life at great speed.
Quickly it eats the insects that have
hatched in the rain … quickly it
finds a mate … quickly it lays its
eggs … the eggs hatch in just one
day … the tadpoles grow so fast
you could see it happening.

By the time the rains are over,
they are young froglets.

Now the Water-holding frogs take
in water through their skins. Soon
they are nearly as round as balls.
Now they are ready to hide from
the dry days and nights.

At this moment, in a desert in Australia,
a frog sleeps. It is deep in a burrow.
It is curled up with its eyes closed.
It is waiting for the rains to fall.

▶ Glossary

 amphibian An amphibian is an animal that lives on land and in water. **7, 8**

 bulge To bulge means to swell outwards. **16**

 burrow A burrow is a hole or tunnel dug by a small animal. **4, 29**

 desert A desert is a dry place with little water where very few plants can grow. **4, 27, 29**

 glide To glide means to float on the air. **5**

 hatch To hatch means to break out of an egg, like a chicken or a tadpole. **20, 28**

marsh A marsh is a wet and watery place where lots of marsh plants grow. **8**

 marsupial A marsupial is an animal which carries its babies in a pouch, like a kangaroo. **6**

 poisonous A poisonous thing has poison in it or on it. Strong poison can kill you. **26**

Reading Together

Oxford Reds have been written by leading children's authors who have a passion for particular non-fiction subjects. So as well as up-to-date information, fascinating facts and stunning pictures, these books provide powerful writing which draws the reader into the text.

Oxford Reds are written in simple language, checked by educational advisors. There is plenty of repetition of words and phrases, and all technical words are explained. They are an ideal vehicle for helping your child develop a love of reading – by building fluency, confidence and enjoyment.

You can help your child by reading the first few pages out loud, then encourage him or her to continue alone. You could share the reading by taking turns to read a page or two. Or you could read the whole book aloud, so your child knows it well before tackling it alone.

Oxford Reds will help your child develop a love of reading and a lasting curiosity about the world we live in.

Sue Palmer
Writer and Literacy Consultant